Overcome Relationship Repetition Syndrome

Why we continually repeat toxic relationship patterns

By Leslie D. Riopel

Author of Amazon Bestsellers

Brain Change to Abundance
Change Everything by Overcoming Fear

Creating Your Own Reality Series

Leslie D Riopel

© Copyright 2012-2014 - Leslie D Riopel

Acknowledgments

To all man and women that seek self improvement

"Walk away from anything or anyone who takes away from your joy. Life is too short to put up with fools." Unknown quote.

Table of Contents

Chapter 1: What in the World is Relationship Repetition Syndrome?.................... 6

Chapter 2: A Toxic Relationship Story.................12

Trapped in a Toxic Cycle.................12

Chapter 3: Toxic Relationship Patterns.................16

Toxic Relationship Quiz.................16

Stuck in the Same Relationship Over and Over.................16

Confronting the Truth Mirror.................18

What Would Your Truth Mirror Reveal to You?.................19

Why do we do this?................. 21

Types of Toxic Relationships – Which One Do You identify With?................. 21

Chapter 4: Discovering Your Inner Child................. 27

Discovering Your Inner Child Self-Reflection Exercise................. 27

Chapter 5: Embracing Your Inner Darkness................. 34

Pushing Out Beyond Your Comfort Zone................. 37

Heart Healing Self-Reflection
Exercise... 44

Chapter 6: Family Relationship Patterns – Why we emulate the one's we love...................................50

Emotional Family
History...51

Chapter 7: Are You Ready for a Healthy Relationship – Moving Into a Space of Love...54

Chapter 8: Meditation for Manifesting Love...59

Disclaimer...66

Refrence...67

Chapter 1: What in the World is Relationship Repetition Syndrome?

"Insanity is repeating the same mistakes and expecting different results"

Is your relationship blissfully happy, loving, delicious, passionate, warm, sweet, trusting, life affirming and filled with joy? If not, why? If you find instead that your relationship is filled with disdain, mistrust, anxiety, stress or jealousy, then you may need to re-examine why you're in it in the first place.

The definition of insanity above is from a Narcotics Anonymous booklet circa1980 - however, one could argue that many of us struggle with the concept of repeating the same mistakes while expecting different results. In the end it doesn't really matter what you are struggling with because if you continue to follow the same old tired path, you will continue to get the same old tired results.

Although the term "Relationship Repetition Syndrome," coined by a Dr. Seth Meyers, may be a new one to you – I'm sure that the idea of continuing to repeat the same toxic relationship patterns is certainly not a new idea for many of us.

What exactly is Relationship Repetition Syndrome you might ask? In short, this syndrome is all about the idea of unconsciously repeating toxic relationship patterns. In other words, you continue to create and recreate the same toxic relationship over and over again, without consciously realizing you are even doing so.

Those suffering from this syndrome might seek out the same kinds of romantic partners over and over again, even if those partners all happen to exhibit the same personality traits that have doomed their relationships in the past.

Now for those of you who have already figured out the relationship thing or those of you who happen to enjoy a beautiful, non-toxic relationship or a relationship that has absolutely no problems whatsoever – this book may not be one you need to read.

However, most of us, myself included, have suffered from this syndrome at one time or another in our lives because it is actually more common than you might think.

Believe me when I say that this is NOT a book written from the perspective of someone who is "preaching" or the perspective of someone who is entrenched in a "perfect" relationship telling you what to do.

This book is meant as a guide to help move you in the right direction and to provide a beacon to those who may have given up hope of ever finding the right relationship.

For those of you who are struggling, know that I am on this journey with you, discovering these secrets myself. I invite you to go on this quest with me, as we figure out how to circumvent these waters and break old habitual patterns that no longer serve us.

Many of us are relationship repeaters – and I would argue that most of us have fallen into this category at one time or another in our lives. Love is one of the most challenging but rewarding emotions known to man, so it makes sense that many of us struggle with it.

I have always envied those people that seem to have it all in terms of relationships. There are those who enjoy beautiful and healthy relationships with seemingly little to no effort - I am not one of them - so don't think I am judging you for being a relationship repeater! While none of us really know what goes on behind closed doors, we all know that relationships take work.

If your relationships feel like you are beating a dead horse over and over, it may be time to admit defeat and it may be time to ask yourself if you are guilty of picking the same kind of flawed partner over and over.

Now I realize all of us are flawed in one way or another, but our relationships don't have to be. There are people who just aren't meant to be together. There are relationships that are toxic. Let's face it - some of us when thrown together are like oil and water. You can mix us up initially and we may be fine for a while, but eventually, we start to come apart. Just like oil and water, it soon takes too much effort to maintain a toxic relationship.

There are many reasons this may happen. People do change and sometimes grow apart. Relationship Repetition Syndrome is all about picking the same kind of partner over and over, while subconsciously knowing that they aren't right for you.

We sometimes revel in our pain and our toxic relationship patterns to the point that we begin to think a toxic relationship is perfectly normal. Other people may see that our relationship is bad, but we often have a hard time seeing that fact ourselves.

I know many people who suffer from this syndrome. They continue to repeat and recycle the same kind of flawed relationship over and over. I even know someone who married the same type of person twice – both times not really realizing he had done so until it was too late.

I recall the conversation Ben and I had quite vividly, it went something like this:

"I spent 16 years in a bad marriage and I really thought that this time it would be different. I thought I was marrying someone completely different than my first wife but I now see that I essentially married the same woman once again, just in a different body."

When Ben as we will call him, married Maggie he thought he had chosen someone new and different than his first wife Carol. He saw personality traits that he liked. He saw someone new and fresh, someone he could grow old with and enjoy spending time with. He thought wrong and it didn't take him long to figure this out. However, by the time he figured it out, it was too late to quickly back out of the relationship because a child was involved. He soon realized that he was right back in the same crappy, relationship he had spent 16 years trying to get out of. Believe me when I say this is not a good thing.

Our relationships should not take so much effort. We shouldn't always be fighting the uphill battle. If you feel as if you are constantly walking around on eggshells, then you may have a problem. Our relationships are supposed to build us up, not suck all the life out of us. In other words, it shouldn't take so much effort.

Now I know that all relationships need nurturing and tending. I'm not saying that they should be "perfect" all of the time, because that would not be realistic. Relationships do take some effort, but they should build you up, not tear you down.

Our worlds are often a mirror reflection of our deepest and innermost thoughts and desires. When we look into this mirror – we see ourselves. This mirror reinforces whatever it is we believe back out into our world.

As Earl Nightingale so beautifully said "We become what we think about."

In other words, our thoughts become things. It really doesn't matter to our mind whether or not we focus on positive things or negative things because this law is always playing out in our lives. We can make whatever we want to make out of our life – we just have to focus on those thoughts and those images that are aligned with the life we wish to live.

The desire to be loved, according to Nightingale, is nothing more than the thought to be loved. If we look into the mirror of our lives and see that we are someone who continually struggles with relationships, then we will continue to struggle with relationships. Until we learn to break through the hurtful self-defeating patterns that hold us back, we will continue to struggle.

Our subconscious thoughts rule our lives. The only person we need to strive to understand in terms of relationships is ourselves - because every single person in our lives is a mirror reflection of our own thoughts and concerns.

If we become that which we think about, what does this mean in terms of relationships? What it means is that everyone is our mirror – that is the great relationship secret.

Each of us is a product of our own reflection. The qualities we most often abhor in other people are often those things that we dislike within ourselves. On the other hand, those qualities that we admire about other people are often those same qualities that we admire within ourselves.

In order to change anything in other words, you must seek to first understand those flaws within yourself. This journey isn't about anyone else but YOU. In order to change the dynamic of a relationship – you must first change yourself. You must first understand yourself. You need to dig deep into those patterns you have subconsciously developed over the course of your life and figure out why you continue to manifest them.

When you begin to understand that certain people were put into your life for a reason or a season – you can then begin to process the hurtful emotions associated with them and you can begin to move forward.

When you take this tour through love and mystery – you are no longer afraid to get hurt. When you begin to understand the concept that each of us is a mirror reflection – you begin to see that you create your own relationship drama. Knowing that you create your own personal experience means that you can also create a new experience – an experience full of love and affection and appreciation.

Acting from the fear of pain doesn't really save you from the pain – it only pushes the pain further down inside you. When you look into this mirror of truth – you begin to see parts of yourself that need to be acknowledged. There is no one staring back in this truth mirror but you – and since your life is a mirror of your thoughts – you have an opportunity to really see yourself for what you really are. With this process, there is no need or room for blame, there is only room for growth.

The repetition of the same old hurtful patterns in your life only means one thing – it means that you have something to learn from the experience. Once you figure out the lesson, you can then move beyond it into a healthy, relationship that nurtures your soul.

This process is akin to opening up the walls of the heart. Often times we put up these self-imposed barriers as a wall of protection. Inside these walls we cannot be hurt – however inside these walls we cannot be loved either.

This process is like peeling an onion – each layer that is removed reveals something new. Each layer you peel back reveals another complexity but also another surprise.

Going through this process sends a message to the universe that you trust in this process and you trust that you will soon be shown the secret to your heart's joy.

I welcome you to take this journey with me – as we strive to discover the secrets of your heart.

Know that as you discover yours, I will also be discovering mine.

Chapter 2: A Toxic Relationship Story

"Consider that you radiate. At all times. Consider that what you're feeling right now is rippling outward into a field of is-ness that anyone can dip their oar into. You are felt. You are heard. You are seen. If you were not here, the world would be different. Because of your presence, the universe is expanding." Danielle LaPorte

Trapped in a Toxic Cycle

Based off of the teaching tales utilized by Milton Erickson, these stories provide a multi-faceted approach to learning.

There once lived a young woman who was trapped in a toxic relationship cycle.

No matter what she did or how hard she tried, she always seemed to end up in the same relationship – only the faces changed. She went to great lengths to select healthy relationships only to ultimately end up in the same one over and over again. She couldn't figure out why this was occurring.

Every relationship she entered into turned out the same – toxic. She once dated a man who drank too much, a man who constantly berated her. She would find herself hiding from this man and hiding from the fact that she was unhappy. She finally worked up the courage to break away from this man only to end up with the same type of man several months later. Every man she attracted – and every man that she found herself drawn to exhibited these same types of characteristics. These men were belligerent, nasty, high-tempered and strong willed, all traits she told herself she couldn't stand. These men were all alcoholics.

"The best and most beautiful things in the world cannot be seen or even touched. They must be felt with the heart." - Helen Keller

Like a moth drawn to a flame, she kept going back to the same relationship, over and over again. She forgot she had the power of choice. She was so invested in this pattern that she

would not look twice at any man who strayed from it. She felt comfort in her pain. She felt as if she didn't really deserve to be happy and peaceful and content. Like a businessman who continues to throw money into a bad investment or a flailing business, she couldn't stop this toxic pattern, no matter how hard she tried.

She told herself that a bad relationship was better than no relationship at all. She told herself that people expected her to be part of a relationship, no matter how bad it was. She was obsessed with trying to fix people and obsessed with rescuing people. She tried to see the good in everyone and was bound and determined to turn these men into someone she could love.

She feared being alone and feared confrontation yet she didn't know why. Her sisters repeated this pattern, selecting men that were hurtful and toxic as well. Her older sister continually chose men who were strong willed, high-tempered and belligerent, yet neither of them could figure out why their relationships were doomed to fail.

Growing up, both sisters had positive role models. Their mother and father were married over fifty years, and they had always been quite happy. Somewhere, somehow both girls had lost the ability to feel and they had lost the ability to stand up for what they so deserved. Deep down, they both felt as if they didn't deserve a healthy loving relationship.

Both women were well educated and very successful. They both had good health and a good education. They had many friends and a loving family, but they just couldn't seem to get out of the cycle of toxicity they were in when it came to relationships.

What they didn't realize was that they were subconsciously choosing men that fit a neat and tidy pattern. They were essentially choosing men that were just like their grandfather Blair. Blair was an alcoholic – but they loved him dearly. They had never known him during the raging alcoholic years while he was drinking - they had only known him as the loving, compassionate family man. Deep down in their hearts, they were continually trying to emulate and attract men just like their grandfather, men who were initially the life of the party and men who loved a good time.

This pattern was buried so deep within the young woman's soul that it took her many years to figure out why she was choosing men that were so wrong for her. She soon realized that she must discover the truth – no matter how much it hurt. She strove to find the answers and she was determined to figure this puzzle out no matter what.

It was within this struggle that she began to finally see the light. She started a movement to help other people who were struggling as well. She discovered the secret to a happy and fulfilling love relationship and this secret lied within herself. The secret she discovered was that everyone was her mirror. Those traits within herself that she abhorred were exactly those traits that she sought out in other people.

The moment she began to see this, was the moment she started to heal. She began to dig down deep within herself to figure out why she kept repeating this pattern. She realized that the solution lied within her. There was no one to blame but herself. She simply needed to love herself more.

In order to begin changing the hurtful dynamic within her relationships, she needed to BE the change she wanted to see. When she could finally start loving herself, faults and all, she finally started to expect more out of her life and more out of herself. The moment she began expecting good things and good people – good people and good things began showing up. Everything was a reflection of her innermost thoughts and feelings.

She began to examine herself in this truth mirror each and every day. She began asking herself a lot of questions, at times she didn't like the answers but she kept digging and kept unearthing raw layer upon layer. She felt raw and exposed but she pursued the process in spite of this.

At times she was terrified of losing herself in another hurtful relationship – but she kept putting herself out there. She learned all about her inner child, and she had an honest conversation with those parts of herself that were holding her back. She examined the relationships emulated within her family and she took the time to heal. Once she worked her way through this process, she began to move into a space of love.

Just like a flower whose buds begin opening up with the light of the sun, she began to reach out to people in friendship and in companionship. She realized that the world was full of good and decent people. She began singing a new song, a song of love and self-respect. Slowly her world started to change as she began opening up her heart.

She began waking up with hope in her heart. She didn't need the pain any longer. She had honest conversations with those people in her life that no longer resonated within her energy. She felt strong enough to speak up. She was finally ready for a healthy relationship.

I urge you to stick with me throughout this process if you see yourself in these words. The steps outlined in this book can help you heal and they can help you move into a healthy and loving relationship. Know that you deserve the best.

"Never regret anything that has happened in your life, it cannot be changed, undone or forgotten so take it as a lesson learned and move on." - Unknown quotes

When life gives you a hundred reasons to cry, show

life that you have a thousand reasons to smile." – Unknown

Chapter 3: Toxic Relationship Patterns

"What you believe is very powerful. If you have toxic emotions of fear, guilt and depression, it is because you have wrong thinking, and you have wrong thinking because of wrong believing."- Joseph Prince

Our relationships often define us. For some, our relationships give us hope while others continue to struggle. Relationships can be our biggest joy, but they can also be our greatest source of sorrow and disappointment. Many of us repeat the same hurtful patterns and mistakes over and over because we are after all only human. Those stuck in a toxic relationship cycle often don't realize they are even in one.

Are you stuck in a toxic relationship cycle? Take this quiz to find out! Answer yes or no.

Toxic Relationship Quiz

1. Do you feel as if everyone you are attracted to is "bad" for you?
2. Do all of your intimate relationships seem difficult and challenging?
3. Do you notice your partners repeating toxic patterns?
4. Are you trying too hard to get it right?
5. Do you rush into relationships?
6. Do you blame yourself when things go wrong?
7. Are you guilty of losing yourself in relationships?

8. Do you feel as if you will never meet someone decent and good?
9. Are you afraid to be alone?
10. Do you always attract the same type of person/personality?

If you answered yes to two or more questions, chances are this syndrome affects you. Relationships shouldn't be so hard, they do take work, we all know that. I am not saying that relationships should not need nurturing or tending, because they do. What I am saying is that your relationship should not be all consuming to the point that your life is unbalanced as a result.

Stuck in the Same Relationship Over and Over

While this book is not written from a doctor's perspective - it is written by someone who understands this pattern - and it is written by someone who understands that thoughts become things. As a Clinical Hypnotherapist with a master's degree, I have seen my fair share of people who continually struggle with one thing or another.

As a woman I understand how challenging relationships can be, but I also understand how rewarding they can be. To love and be loved is the greatest honor and one we should all have the privilege of experiencing at some point in our lives.

Many of us are relationship recycler's or relationship repeaters. While some strive to breathe life into old relationships or relationships of the past others simply seek the same type of partner over and over. Why do we do this?

I can cite many examples of people I know that have suffered from this syndrome. I have one friend, a man, who has struggled with this for years. He is immersed in a whirlwind of chaos, and all of the women he chooses follow the same type of toxic pattern. Every relationship he has been in for the past several years has been toxic. Now I don't know why he keeps choosing the same type of partner, but I am empathetic because I have done the same thing myself.

My sister, who has finally broken away from this pattern, chose the same type of men for years. She chose men who were controlling and domineering. When her marriage broke up many years ago, she spent a long time alone trying to evaluate why she kept choosing the wrong type of man. When she was finally ready to seek love again, she found someone she thought was a great guy. She actually ended up marrying this great guy after only a few months of dating. In the end, she was right back where she started, and their relationship came to a screeching halt the moment this violent abusive man pulled a gun on her.

As if this weren't enough, she spent the next few years really being careful of the men she chose. When she was ready to date once again, she made a special point to choose someone who didn't seem to fit her relationship mold. Most of the men she had dated were good looking men with great hair, so she made a special point to choose a bald man the next time. I'm here to tell you that hair doesn't make a person good or bad, because this new man was just as destructive as the old men were. She actually tried to choose someone much different than she had ever chosen. She chose someone who was a family man and someone with a steady job. She thought he was a good fit. In the end, this man became violent and abusive as well and he was also a drug addict. Many of these characteristics were probably characteristics she disliked within herself, because she herself tends to have a very addictive personality.

What is it that causes us to continually repeat these hurtful patterns? Why are relationships so difficult for some yet so easy for others? Why is it that bright, energetic and talented individuals continue to choose partners that are so wrong for them? Much like a compulsion like OCD, it is very hard to break away from a comfortable pattern. We like patterns because they are familiar. We are often afraid to break out of a cycle because we find solace and comfort in our pain and agony. Deep down there is a reason we choose to stay stuck.

Once we begin to understand that our relationships are a mirror, we can then begin to analyze why we continue to manifest the same destructive patterns over and over.

Confronting the Truth Mirror

We can probably all recall the story of Snow White and the Seven Dwarves. Snow White was a beautiful girl with lips as red as blood and hair as black as ebony. Her fair skin was white as snow - hence the book's title Snow White.

When Snow White's birth mother died after giving birth, the King married a new woman. This woman became Snow White's stepmother. She studied dark magic and owned a magic mirror, in which she would ask daily:

"Mirror, mirror on the wall, who's the fairest of them all?"

Each time she would ask the mirror this question, the mirror would reply:

"Thou, O Queen, art the fairest of all."

The queen was always quite pleased with this reply, because she knew her mirror could only speak the truth.

The story continues without event until one day the queen asked once again:

"Mirror, mirror on the wall, who's the fairest of them all?" Needless to say, she was quite shocked when it answered:

"You, my queen, are fair; it is true. But Snow White is even fairer than you."

Anyone familiar with this story knows that this reply sent the Queen into a jealous rage. The Queen then ordered her huntsman to take Snow White into the woods and she ordered them to kill Snow White so that she could then again be the fairest of them all. The Queen also demanded that the huntsman return with Snow White's heart as proof.

The poor huntsman, being a kind and gentle man, took Snow White into the forest, but soon found himself unable to kill the girl letting her go instead, bringing the Queen the heart of a wild boar.

We know that Snow White comes out fine in the end but in light of this story, it may behoove us to ask ourselves the question of what our mirror of truth would reveal, if we had one to stand in front of.

What Would Your Truth Mirror Reveal to You?

"Each of us is merely a reflection of our inner most thoughts and desires."

Imagine right now that you could stand in front of your very own mirror of truth. What would it be like to be completely up front and honest with yourself, as it pertains to love and relationships? Are you truly happy with the person you are? Are there things about yourself that displease you? If so, ask yourself why. Where do these feelings of discontentment come from? What were the messages you received growing up? Were they positive or negative?

Messages perceived by us as a child can have life-long consequences.

Each of us carries around a lot of emotional baggage. This baggage weighs us down. For someone experiencing a pattern of dysfunctional relationships, there are no easy answers. However, a good place to start is to start by looking at the relationship role models you had a child.

Sigmund Freud spoke of something called a "repetition compulsion" which is essentially a defense mechanism and something we do to try and rewrite history per se. For those who continually experience hurtful relationships, the history that is attempting to be rewritten might be a troubled relationship with an opposite sex parent for example. However, there may be other troubled relationships one is emulating as well.

When the message you received as a child was about abandonment, rejection, frustration, neglect, abuse or disappointment for example,you might create a certain set of circumstances as a child to emotionally deal with this. You might for example cling to the hope that if you were only smarter, prettier, funnier, quieter, thinner or anything else, that you would finally win over mom or dad - or whoever it might be - until they finally lovedyou as you needed them to love you – unconditionally.

Many of us blame ourselves when we shouldn't - and this creates a whole new set of problems going forward. Now no one is perfect of course so everyone experiences this to some extent. James Masterson, a psychoanalyst, termed the phrase "abandonment depression" which translates to the hope of being able to change the parent's response by becoming what we perceive he or she would want us to be.

As long as we still cling to that hope, we keep ourselves from sinking into complete and total despair. As adults, we continue this pattern unconsciously superimposing it onto the people that come into our lives.

As humans we tend to seek comfort in the familiar. Our desire to return to the past is so strong that we often continue repeating these hurtful destructive patterns into our adult life. While Freud believed that as humans we continually revisit harmful behaviors because of the comfort factor, there may be other reasons why we do this.

Many of the patterns we develop as children get ingrained or burned into our minds so much so that we don't even realize it. We create a shield around ourselves that protects us from harm. These internal maps or subjective thought patterns become our entire world. When we become stressed or worried or angry, we return to what feels safe.

We do what we have always done, return to the scene of the crime within our minds. In other words, we keep manifesting the same type of situation that we are comfortable with, even if it's not a good one.

The only way to escape this tendency is to first identify and then examine why you are doing this. Reaching deep into yourself and accessing that inner child can help you further understand why you keep creating the same destructive condition or relationship over and over.

Why do we do this?

The classic story "Snow White" serves as a very powerful metaphorical symbol, because it helps you to make better more conscious decisions. This story helps you realize that you are in control of your life, you and only you. You have the power of choice, just like Snow White did when she chose to bite the apple. The wicked witch represents negative influences society throws at us, but it also humbles us when we see the witch's vulnerable side, the side of her that feels that she does not deserve love or happiness or joy.

The prince represents positive influences in our life and divine transformation. The prince gives us hope and joy and inspiration. Each of the seven dwarves can represent a part of your personality as well as you experience the happiness and joy and the emotional burdens the characters go through.

Types of Toxic Relationships – Which One Do You identifywith?

"Everything in your life has prepared you for what is to come. Don't try and make something happen - allow it to happen."

We all want connections in our lives because it's nice to be loved and touched and desired. Let's face it - life is much better when shared with someone you love. While none of us are perfect by any means, there are some people or shall I say combinations of people that are more difficult than others. Sometimes those difficulties stem from being with someone who is just not right for you. Just like the oil and water analogy we talked about previously, some people just don't gel well when put together.

Even the best relationships take work – however, your intimate relationship should build you up, not tear you down. If you are constantly feeling like you are under a microscope and always having to defend your actions, you may want to reconsider if the relationship you are in is the right one for you.

There are some common types of toxic relationship or relationship patterns we can look at. You may resonate with some of these, or you may not.

The Belittler

This type of person is constantly berating or belittling you. This type of partner will belittle you anywhere, whether you are in public or private. If you are with someone who does this, and you have asked him or her to stop and they haven't, that may be a warning sign that they don't want to change. This type of partner may even make you feel as if you are "lucky" to have them. Anyone who tolerates this behavior will soon find themselves feeling like a victim.

Relating this to my own life, I can now see that I was once with someone who was the classic belittler. He would berate me any chance he got. He was also a severe alcoholic. He would sit in my little kitchen and tell me what a filthy housekeeper and cook I was. Why I put up with this, I don't know. All of this behavior was coming from a man who still lived at home with his mother - that should have been my first clue. While David was certainly blessed in the looks department, he failed on every other level. His story has a rather sad ending, as I found out years later that he had shot himself by accident during one of his drinking binges. He did this while arguing with his mother at their home. It's a very sad story and I was sorry to hear it. However, I was glad I got out of the relationship when I did.

I can clearly see now how destructive this behavior was, but I couldn't see it then. Don't beat yourself up if you find yourself in this type of relationship, because believe me when I say, I have been there!

The Bad Temper

While all of us experience times in our lives when we are in a bad mood, someone with this type of toxic pattern may try and control by intimidation. Someone with a hair-trigger temper or someone with a short fuse will be difficult no matter what. This type of behavior is very draining, because you will soon find yourself walking around on eggshells, being careful not to do anything that might set them off.

This type of person will probably not show this side of himself or herself off to the world, so you may have a hard time explaining to people why you cannot tolerate this kind of person. It doesn't do any good to try and explain to this kind of partner that you do not like the angry outbursts, because they will most likely blame their behavior on you. This kind of behavior where someone does not own his or heractions can be very difficult to live with.

I once lived with a man everyone called "LC" for loose cannon. I can tell right now that is not an endearing term. My uncle named him that because he had a hair trigger temper. Living with him was difficult at best. He was also part Algonquin Indian, which may or may not have had something to do with his temper. The alcohol he constantly drank only exacerbated his temper. I was so terrified of this man that I had to have my father come over and help me break up with him. I wasn't sure how he would take it. I recall that he locked himself in our spare room for weeks until I could get him to move out and move on. If you find yourself with someone who constantly has a bad temper, do yourself a favor, and move on.

The Guilt Inducer

The guilt inducer works by inducing guilt in the victim. This kind of person controls you by making you feel guilty at every opportunity. They might do this by telling you how disappointed they are with your behavior or they might even remove guilt if you do what they want. This will only make you feel better temporarily.

This is a very common behavior and form of control that parent's often use on their children to get them to complete tasks. As with all toxic behaviors, this kind of behavior is designed to control you. This is the only way the guilt inducer knows how to operate. The best plan of action is to simply stand firm in your convictions. Be strong and don't fall prey to their ploys. If you are with someone who constantly makes you feel guilty, it may be time to move on.

The Over-Reactor

The over reactor is someone who makes a mountain out of a molehill if you know what I mean. You may find yourself comforting this type of person in order to deal with their constant over reactions. If you have ever tried to tell someone that you are unhappy or displeased with their actions, and they in turn make you feel worse, you may be dealing with an over reactor.

This type of person may also be guilty of deflecting and making you feel as if everything is your fault. This is another classic toxic behavior.

The Over-Dependent

Someone who is overly dependent wants you to make each and every decision for them. They may be passive and afraid to make their own decisions. This kind of person may also be passive-aggressive, and they will definitely let you know when you have made a decision they are not happy with.

If you are with someone who pouts or doesn't speak to you for days, they may be guilty of this behavior. Believe it or not, being passive is a very powerful method of control! This kind of person can leave you feeling very drained, because in the end it's just too much work trying to cater to their every need.

The Independent Controller

On the other end of the scale, we have the classic overly independent partner. This person doesn't want anyone controlling them. They may leave you in the dark as to what their plans are and they also be very evasive. They are very unpredictable and unreliable. It's nearly impossible to make plans with this kind of person because they will never commit to anything.

I have been with someone who falls into this category and I can tell you from personal experience that it was utterly exasperating. This kind of person will always keep you guessing and this may leave you with so much anxiety, that it's not even worth being in the relationship. This in itself is simply another method of control.

The User

The user is great, assuming they are getting everything they want from you. However, you can never do enough for the user, and this can be a huge energy drainer. They may tease you on occasion by doing something small for you, but they won't do this very often. When this does happen, you will feel obligated to pay them back.Being in a relationship with this kind of person is draining at best.

The Paranoid/Possessive Partner or the Control Freak

This kind of person will drive you crazy with their possessiveness. In the end, this kind of person may just be the worst kind of person to be with. This type of toxic person may be extremely jealous, which may be endearing initially. They may even tell you that once you are in a committed relationship with them, that they will not be so possessive, however, you shouldn't believe them!

This kind of person becomes more and more suspicious as time goes on. They might even check the mileage on your car to see how far you've gone which is ridiculous. If you stay out late they may interrogate you and make you feel awful. In the end, you will most likely end up with no friends left at all, because this kind of paranoid person suspects everyone. Any effort to reassure someone like this will go unnoticed. Staying in this kind of relationship will mean you will eventually have no life of your own.

I once dated a man who was so possessive that after I broke up with him he hung out in my tree in the back yard waiting for my date and I to come home. Now this is certainly not normal behavior by any means. If someone doesn't trust you, they will never trust you so you are probably better off being alone, than being with someone who is extremely jealous or possessive.

These kinds of behaviors can serve as warning signs. Having said that, it doesn't mean you have to give up on someone if they show these kinds of signs every now and then. There are different levels of toxic behaviors, and everyone has their own standard; if someone cares for you and they are willing to change or compromise, they may be worth fighting for, only you can be the judge.

"If you could only see how beautiful the light of your spirit shines - you would never be sad."

Chapter 4: Discovering Your Inner Child

"Some things can only be understood when you're in a tree house. With a pile of warm chocolate chip cookies. And a book." ~Dr. SunWolf, professorsunwolf.com

If you do not believe in yourself or believe that you deserve a loving and healthy relationship, then it will be difficult for you to receive love. This process is like peeling an onion – each layer that is removed reveals more clues and more of that inner raw surface. Before you can change this dynamic, you have to dig down deep inside yourself and ask yourself why you continue to repeat hurtful patterns.

Our inner child can reveal so much; many of our problems as adults stem from things that happened as a child. All of our fears, insecurities and beliefs travel with us into adulthood where we continue creating the same world over and over again.

This exercise to discover your inner child is simple, yet life changing.

Discovering Your Inner Child Self-Reflection Exercise

Just like before, you may stop anywhere along the way to pause and reflect but there are suggested areas where you can stop and reflect as well. You may choose to read each passage, stopping to visualize the suggestions along the way, or you may choose to read through the entire piece first, then go back to do the exercise. Do whatever feels comfortable for you.

You might take a seat on the floor – on a rug or a soft pillow. Take a few deep breaths to clear your energy.

Now imagine you are in a beautiful and tranquil space – you might envisionwhite candles or other relaxing images surrounding you. Breathe in the energy of love – the energy of self-love. Visualize the color of this self-love now, it might be a soft pink or green or even a crème or white, whatever feels right for you.

Absorb this energy and notice what it feels like to really love yourself right here in this moment for exactly who you are – flaws and all.

You areincredibly loved – by everyone so it's time to love yourself with this same kind of love and compassion. Now imagine a kind of internal flame within the energy of your body. Feel the heat of the flame against your skin.

Imagine or will this internal flame to rise - and notice how it feels as it expands all around you. Feel how nice it feels to be so safe and warm, so protected and so loved.

Spend a few moments doing this before moving on to the next section.

Now imagineyou are traveling back in time, to a time when you perhaps didn't feel love for yourself. Think back to where it all started – this feeling that you weren't good enough or special enough or deserving enough.

This might be a key event or time or just a feeling you recall – it doesn't matter. Ask your inner child to present itself now - but ask kindly and gently.

Imagine you are meeting a part of you from your past that needs a little extra love or encouragement. Think of yourself as your older, caring self and this part of you that needs more encouragement as your inner child.

This part of your personality still plays a role today and your inner child might be a key reason as to why you keep creating and recreating the same situations or relationships.

Take yourself back to a time when you felt hurt or disappointed in some way. This could be something big that happened, or even something small; it doesn't matter how small or how big the event was, it all has meaning.

Ask your mind to reveal this event now. Be patient – sometimes you need to quiet your mind in order to identify this root cause.

As your inner child approaches –notice how you feel. Do you feel strong and empowered or small and weak? Notice how old you are and even what you are wearing. Feel the energy of your inner child and sit in quiet contemplation for a while.

You might find it helpful to imagine yourself walking in the woods or along the beach with your inner child, just enjoying each other's company. Sometimes words are not even necessary.

Spend a few moments connecting with your inner child before moving on to the next section.

Now begin speaking with your younger self. Ask them why they feel hurt or scared or disappointed. Ask them why they don't feel that they deserve a loving and healthy relationship. Examine the feelings and the reasoning behind your motivation.

It's OK to be sad, or angry or even hurt. You are seeing this event from an adult's perspective now. It's time to heal – it's time to love.

Approach your inner child, like a caring adult would, with love and compassion. This part of you needs reassurance that everything is fine - and you are going to offer this reassurance.

Now try kneeling down and coming face to face in your mind with this inner child within you. Look eye to eye with love and compassion. As you do so, offer your inner child kindness and reassurance, because that is what your inner child craves.

Now tell your inner child that everything is going to be fine. Everything turned out great. Tell this inner child that you totally and absolutely love him or her from the deepest level of your soul.

Kindly tell your inner child that you totally and absolutely love them and that you believe in them. Tell your inner child that they are loved and they deserve to be loved. Tell them there is nothing wrong with them – and that they are perfect in every way. Tell them they are deeply loved and they deserve the best. Tell them they should expect everything from their life – including an incredibly fulfilling and passionate love relationship.

As you speak to this inner child, this younger version of you, you may feel emotional, and that's OK. Let it all out, there is no one here but you. Let your emotions out. It's time to heal. It is time to feel the love you have for yourself.

Spend a few moments here before moving on to the next section.

Now forgive anyone and everyone may have hurt you. Release the bitterness and the anger, if there is any. Bless everyone you have ever come in contact with and send them light and love. Anger and bitterness only hold you back – it's time to let it all go. Ask yourself – and your inner child – if there is anything you need to release – if there is anything that doesn't serve you now.

You may recall feelings of abandonment, shame, guilt, fear, rejection, frustration, neglect, abuse or even disappointment for example. See yourself in a key moment – and again ask this inner child why they feel like they don't deserve a healthy and loving relationship. Ask them what is behind their motivation.

As you stand with this inner child, again notice how you feel. Do you feel happiness and joy? Do you feel ashamed or embarrassed? Speak with your inner child and examine the emotion of love. Think back to how you viewed love as a child? Did the adults around you express love in a healthy manner? If not - ask yourself why?

Spend a few moments reflecting until something comes to your mind that makes sense. For example, if you are afraid to stand up to people, you may see yourself as a child cowering in the corner. You may see a certain event that caused this. Perhaps someone yelled at you or caused you to experience fear. Ask yourself if there is someone in your earlier life that may have caused this.

Now imagine and feel the hurtful energy leaving your body – moving out into time and space. Feel the colors change as you release this negative energy. Feel how much lighter you feel being freed from this energy.

Tell your younger self that everything is going to be fine. Hug your inner child. Feel the love between you and your inner child.

This love and this encouragement will take root and begin to grow and expand. Slowly and surely you will begin to heal. This positive and loving attitude towards yourself will outshine and heal your feeling of somehow not being good enough, or special enough.

As you begin to heal, the emptiness and the loneliness that comes from not loving yourself enough will begin to fade.

Now ask yourself what you need to do to fully accept and love yourself right here in this moment? What are the conditions you place upon yourself? Think about those now. What if all of that didn't matter – what if all of that could be healed by the simple act of love – of just loving yourself – in spite of yourself, and mostly because of yourself?

Pause.....

Now that you have identified these additional "conditions" let them all go. Release them out into the world, for they serve absolutely no purpose. See yourself engaged in a loving and healthy relationship. See yourself standing up to those people in your life that no longer serve you.

If you would like, imagine someone in your life right now that you could benefit from speaking to. See them appearing before you right now. This could be someone you are angry with, someone you need to merely express love to or someone you just need to be brutally honest with.

Express your inner most feelings in your mind straight to this person. Be very clear. If you are upset with someone from your past – you may envision them here as well. Take as long as you need to clear your energy.

Watch as all of this hurtful energy leaves your body and your spirit and watch as the energy is transformed by the love all around you.

Spend a few moments here before moving on to the next section.

Loving yourself creates a firm foundation for your life. Now examine your standards as it pertains to love and relationships. Ask yourself how high your standards really are. Think about those qualities you seek in a loving relationship or what kind of personality you look for. If you are already in a loving relationship, think about those ways that you could express your love more kindly and more genuinely.

Relationships are always ebbing and flowing, so they require care. Ask your inner child how he or she views the world? Do they view it as a loving, giving place - if not, ask them why?

Wrap your arms around your inner child once again and ask them what they need from you in order to experience love more deeply and more openly and honestly. If you are seeking love, try and see yourself from an outside perspective. Do you resonate the energy of love? Are you open to love and companionship? Are you a good receiver of love? If not, you can change that dynamic.

Notice what kind of energetic vibrations you put out - are you open and appreciative, or closed off and silent? Use this time to examine your viewpoints on love. If you met yourself for the first time, what image would you take away? Take a moment to truly become aware of your own energy.

Embrace yourself and your life - flaws and all. Your flaws make you unique and special. Now give yourself "permission" to love yourself, no matter what. You are enough, and you have enough and you CAN have it all.

Make a pact to be kinder to yourself and to treat yourself with more love and respect.

Repeat the following statement....

"I am unique and I am me. There is no one else in the world quite like me. I have a very unique blend of skills and talents. I own everything about me. I am kind and loveable. I accept myself for exactly who I am in this moment in time. I deserve love because I am love."

Now just sit and meditate on your worthiness as long as you like and give yourself a mental hug. Feel the warmth and the joy and the compassion. Feel the love all around you. This love surrounds you like a warm glow. Imagine a pink glow of energy surrounding you – emanating from your heart. Breathe in and out and watch how the sphere expands and contracts. Picture the color of your breath as it goes in and of your lungs. Stay here as long as you like.

Chapter 5: Embracing Your Inner Darkness

"We all need to look into the dark side of our nature that's where the energy is, the passion. People are afraid of that because it holds pieces of us we're busy denying." - Sue Grafton

If everyone is our mirror, then we have to stop and ask ourselves what qualities someone has that emulate ours. These are often the darkest parts of our soul. Many of us, myself included, would rather not acknowledge or examine these dark parts, but it is a necessary evil nonetheless.

"We all have a dream in our hearts. If you have not discovered yours it's never too late. Trust that your destiny is unfolding exactly as it is supposed to in the perfect time in the perfect way because you are amazing."

The next step in this process involves reaching deep down inside yourself and pulling out the weeds. This part of ourselves is otherwise known as "the evil monster" within. We all have an evil monster – however, some of us might go our entire lives without examining it.

Each of us has a good side and a bad side. We show our good side to the world, our bad side stays hidden. When you are dating someone you make a special effort to always show your good side, your perfect side. However, like the yin and the yang, what comes up must also come down. Sooner or later your evil monster is tired of hiding. You try and push the evil monster deep down within your soul so that it is deeply hidden. This only works for a while though.

45

There is always a part of you within that likes the darkness. When you are embroiled in a difficult relationship or you find yourself repeating the same kind of relationships over and over to no avail – you might need to stop and ask yourself what's in it for you. This is where the concept of a secondary gain comes into play. In other words, the evil monster within is getting some kind of pleasure or reward when you continue this behavior. The trick is figuring out what it is.

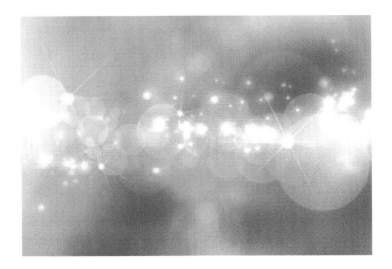

"If we had no winter, the spring would not be so pleasant: if we did not sometimes taste of adversity, prosperity would not be so welcome." - Meditations Divine and Moral"

Each of us has a judgmental, nasty, bitter, jealous, high-tempered, angry or resentful part of us whether we admit it or not. Usually this part of us comes out when we are immersed in a destructive relationship. Since everyone is our mirror, they are merely emulating those qualities we don't like within ourselves.

An example of this would be someone who is motivated, talented, energetic and goal driven finding themselves in a relationship with someone who has the motivation of a sloth. Deep down inside, there is a part of us that doesn't feel so motivated – a part of us that grows tired of always being so driven or focused. We don't necessarily like this part of us. Because we push this part of our personality deep down inside, someone comes along that openly displays it and we are drawn in, we just don't know why.

We then find ourselves complaining about how much we despise this person – but for some reason we can't pull away. Our evil monster likes having a buddy so there is a secondary gain we are deriving.

When you can learn to embrace the darkness within, you are challenged to stop and look within so that you may analyze your own darker side.

There is always a part of our consciousness that lies in the murky waters of our soul. If you can shine a spotlight on those parts and dig them out – you can begin to understand them better. What you may find are some deep-seated insecurities or a deep-seated need for approval. Some of these tendencies may in fact stem from childhood issues or from your tendency to always seek approval from an authority figure. This is akin to finding that secondary gain.

The dark side of your personality may not necessarily be evil – but it does in fact need to be recognized and acknowledged.

We need to embrace this darkness in order to move forward. The dark side can help us defend ourselves, avoid negativity and even help us stand up for what we believe in. When you can examine and acknowledge the dark side, you become much more balanced.

Everything in nature is balanced. Without pain, we would not recognize pleasure. Without the dark, we would not see the light. Just like a dark force within, these energies are necessary in our lives.

If a part of you is continually running from the pain and running from the truth – this part of you will eventually surface and demand to be acknowledged.

At each stage of our lives, there are countless traumas. These events can keep us from resolving issues. If these issues continue to be unresolved, they stay with us throughout our lives, often expressing themselves within our relationships both with ourselves and others.

Those of us that find ourselves experiencing unhealthy relationship patterns, low self-esteem, addictions and the like may actually be experiencing unresolved issues from our childhood. These evil monsters may rear their ugly heads again and again until we stand up and greet them.

Most of the time we make more out of a situation or a fear than we need to – as a result the negative emotions engulf us. We end up in a suffocating in a well of grief, pain, sadness, disappointment, and anger until it becomes a swirling mass of negativity.

Pushing Out Beyond Your Comfort Zone

Forgiveness – Moving Beyond Self-Imposed Barriers

I love this photo because it is the perfect depiction of our fears. It is very hard to step out of your comfort zone. We like our comfort zones because they are safe. We stay within our comfort zones so much so that we hold ourselves back from experiencing new things in life.

Sometimes one cannot step out of their zone of comfort until they learn how to heal their heart. Everything that has ever happened to us sits within the energy of our heart. If you have ever studied anything metaphysical, you have probably heard of the term chakra at one time or another.

The chakra system consists of seven main levels that correspond to various systems of the body. The word chakra comes from the ancient

Sanskrit word "Wheel." The chakras are located not in your physical body, but in your ethereal body, even though they relate to the systems in your physical body.

The chakras are shaped like a flower or a wheel, with petals or spokes that detail their composition. The chakras contain and process energy in your body and just as energy can propel you it can also block you. The chakras act like spinning balls of energy within your body and you could think of them like a series of cogs running up and down your spine, continuously renewing your energy.

In a well-balanced person and in a person who experiences healthy relationships, the chakras would most likely spin rapidly and smoothly. If you could visualize them their colors would be clear and bright. When you are stressed or ill or mentally impaired in any way, your chakras tend to get stuck and they may begin to slow down or spin too quickly, they can even get discolored or fragmented if you are mentally, emotionally or physically impaired. None of us are perfect, so we all experience some kind of chakra imbalance some of the time, however, the aim of chakra healing is to get all of the chakras working and spinning smoothly and evenly, helping you to re-balance your energy.

These energy systems of the body can help you or hurt you, depending on how they are spinning. In order to be healthy and happy you must balance each chakra to properly align your energy. Once you balance each chakra, both the emotional issue as well as the corresponding physical issues should be relieved. Once you understand this energy, you will be able to bring power and balance back into your life so that you may live a joyful and healthy life.

The heart chakra, which is the fourth chakra, sits at the exact center of this beautiful energy system. The Glandular connection is the thymus, which is responsible for building a strong immunity from pain and disease.

The physical location of the heart chakra is in the middle of the chest above your heart. The heart chakra rules relationships and matters of the heart. While other chakras may also play a role when it comes to love and relationships, the heart chakra plays the biggest role.

The body parts affected by the heart chakra are the heart, lungs, pericardium, and circulation. The 4th chakra is usually associated with the color green and it is associated with the element air. The heart chakra is also called the Anahata chakra. Emotionally, the heart chakra affects your experience of love for yourself and others.

This chakra allows you to feel joy, compassion, and peace and it enriches your relationships. A healthy 4th chakra allows you to love deeply, feel compassion and have a deep sense of peace and centeredness. To experience the magic of the heart chakra, you may enjoy imagining yourself in the center of a beautiful chamber, surrounded by the color green. Some enjoy imaging the color pink as well.

Releasing built up energy in the heart chakra allows you to dissolve any hurts, or anger or resentments you may be holding, because those things hold you back. Some even enjoy envisioning the energy of the heart as a beautiful flower, whose petals open and close.

When working with the chakras and especially the heart chakra, one may move the colors up and down their body and envision the colors as a spinning wheel, spinning away any impurities or blockages that may exist, allowing the energy of love to take over.

Clearing away the negativity and the bitterness can work miracles when it comes to overcoming negative and limiting relationship patterns.

The chakras are a beautiful energetic system within your body. You may use them to heal yourself of any emotional imbalances. Chakras pull energy in from your environment, distributing this energy within your body - so that is why it is necessary to cleanse your chakras on a regular basis.

Each chakra spirals down into the body and has many layers. The top layer receives energy from recent events, and this energy can sometimes weigh you down. Clearing your chakras can remove this toxic energy helping you to manage difficult life events much better. When the chakras are healthy, they spin in a clockwise motion and their colors are pure and clear. You can clear your energy merely by imagining your chakras as spinning balls of energy radiating out from your body. If you picture a clock face out resting on your chakras, you can spin the chakra energies clockwise, clearing away any emotional debris.

Before we move on to a heart chakra healing exercise, let's briefly review what the other six chakras are responsible for.

The 1st chakra is known as the Root Chakra or Muladhara chakra.

The root chakra is usually a beautiful deep shade of red, and it connects you to the earth and to your survival instinct. The root chakra is located at the base of the spine, forming your foundation and your physical orientation to self-preservation. Ideally this chakra brings one health, prosperity, security, and a dynamic presence.

The best way to connect to the root chakra is to imagine yourself connected to a long intertwining system of roots, which connects you to the earth. It's important that you feel connected and safe and secure, and the root chakra helps you to do that. You may even enjoy imagining yourself in a beautiful temple on the ground floor as you connect with your root chakra. Imagine this chamber is a beautiful deep shade of red and envision this color washing over you. Ground yourself into the earth and visualize this beautiful color penetrating every cell in your body, connecting you to Mother Earth. Imagine the color has now formed a wheel at the base of your spine and spin the color clockwise now so that it can realign your energy, helping you to feel more grounded.

The 2nd chakra is known as the Sacral or Swadhisthana chakra.

The Sacral chakra is located in the abdomen, lower back and sexual organs. It is related to the element water, and has to do with your emotions and sexuality. It connects you to others through feelings, desires, sensations, and movements.

Ideally this chakra brings youresilience and grace, sexual fulfillment, and the ability to more easily accept change. The second chakra is usually represented by the color orange. The glandular connection is the ovaries or testes, which controls sexual development and reproduction. You may imagine that you are in the 2nd level of this beautiful temple or chamber, envisioning the color orange all around you. Now imagine this color as a beautiful stream, and move the stream of color all around your body, washing it gently. Water is cleansing and peaceful and calm, just like the 2nd chakra. Imagine the color as a beautiful spinning wheel and move it clockwise so it spins out any impurities, connecting you to this river of life.

The 3rd chakra is known as the solar plexus chakra or Manipura chakra.

The physical location of the solar plexus chakra is in the stomach region. The glandular connection is the pancreas, which controls digestion and processes sugar. The 3rd chakra is associated with the color yellow.

Emotionally, the solar plexus chakra affects your self-worth, confidence, personal power, and freedom of choice. The third chakra is your power chakra and it rules your personal power, will, and autonomy, as well as your metabolism. When healthy, this chakra brings you energy, effectiveness, spontaneity, and non-dominating power and is related to the element fire.

You may enjoy imagining you are in the 3rd level of this beautiful chamber, envisioning the color yellow all around you. Let this color wash over you, like a powerful fire, burning away any imbalances or fears or doubts that may exist. Let the color melt away any blockages that you see, and ask your mind to help you release anything that does not support your optimal health. Envision the color like a wheel again, spinning and moving it, so that it may realign your energy.

The 5th chakra is the throat chakra or Vishuddha chakra.

The physical location of the throat chakra is of course the throat. The glandular connection is the thyroid, which controls metabolism; this chakra also affects physical and mental development. The body parts affected by the throat chakra are the throat, mouth, teeth, jaw and ears.

The 5th chakra is associated with the color blue and it is associated with the element ether, in which all things are contained. Emotionally, the throat chakra affects your ability to express yourself, which includes releasing emotions by crying, shouting, and even laughing. The 5th chakra is also the chakra that is also related to communication and creativity. Here you experience the world symbolically through vibration, such as the vibration of sound representing language.

To experience the 5th chakra, you may imagine you are lighting a beautiful candle to illuminate this chakra, surrounding yourself with a soft blue color. Let this color become a wheel, and again spin it so it releases all that does not support you, and let the real truth of your convictions shine.

The 6th chakra is the brow or third eye chakra, known as the Ajna chakra.

This chakra represents light, your higher mind, your intuition, and your imagination. The physical location of the brow chakra is between the eyebrows and it is related to your intuition and your act of seeing, both physically and intuitively. The 6th chakra is associated with the pituitary gland, which influences things like growth and metabolism and hormones.

The 6th chakra is associated with the color indigo and it is associated with the cosmos. This chakra is a lighter and faster vibration and it connects you to your intuition. This chakra allows you to create your visions and make them real, helping you to manifest your desires. To experience the magic of this chakra, take a moment to think about what it is that you desire, and let this chakra help you do so. Now light a beautiful candle and let the color indigo wash over you, and then spin it clockwise, helping you move your desires out into the physical realm.

The 7th chakra is the crown chakra, the thousand-petal lotus or Sahasrara chakra.

This chakra acts as the operating system of the chakras. The physical location of the crown chakra is the top of the head. The glandular connection is the pineal gland, which produces melatonin and regulates your body clock.

The 7th chakra is associated with the color violet, but it can be any color that feels right. Its associated element is also the cosmos, the same as the 6th chakra. Emotionally this chakra is only able to experience the feeling of bliss. Once you have transcended through the other energy centers, all other negative emotions are negated and you feel a joyful sense of oneness with the divine.

The crown chakra relates to consciousness and pure awareness. It is your connection to the greater world beyond, to a timeless, space-less place of allknowing. When developed, this chakra brings you knowledge, wisdom, understanding, spiritual connection, and bliss. This chakra connects you to the universal energy of all existence.

Take a moment now to envision this chakra seeing it like a light streaming in from above, moving the color all through your body. Light a beautiful candle now in your mind and see if there is anything that needs to be cleansed. Turn the color into a beautiful multi-colored wheel and spin it so that it connects to every other chakra, cleansing your body of any toxins or damage that may be present.

This next exercise is a wonderful exercise to help you heal the heart.

While there may be many methods and exercises you can do to overcome something like Relationship Repetition Syndrome, nothing is more effective than examining your own personal needs and motivations. Once you begin to examine the energy of the heart chakra, you can then begin to further understand and unravel the complex energy within.

Many of our emotional blocks stem from the chakras – especially the heart chakra. A lifetime of hurts and emotional turmoil often sits within the energy of the heart.

Examining this and acknowledging the energy of the heart is a wonderful place to start. You might be surprised at how effective this simple little exercise is. The first time I did this, I was shocked at how I felt. While this meditation does not seem very involved, it can pull up some very strong energy within. When I did this exercise for the first time, I felt angry and nervous. The energy within me was very strong. I was uncomfortable at first, because I don't typically like confrontation or pain. I sat with the energy for quite a while, simply acknowledging its presence.

You may need to repeat this exercise time and time again. When I first started meditating with the energy of the heart, I realized I had a lot of pain that needed to come out. I felt the energy within me like a knot tightened around my heart. The harder I pulled, the tighter the knot became. It took a lot of time and effortuntil I could start visualizing another solution. I began to allow the energy of the heart to loosen its grip on the knot. Slowly but surely, the knot began to unravel.

You may see the energy around your heart as something different, maybe as some kind of shackle or chain even – don't be scared or nervous, just learn to sit with the image as long as you can. Eventually, your mind will lead you to a solution that allows you to loosen its grip. You may see the knot unraveling, you may get a key to unlock the chain or you may imagine the energy being washed away by the healing movement of water.

You may choose to work with a healing stone like a rose quartz crystal if you have access to one, placing it on your chest during the meditation. You may also simply visualize a healing stone, if you don't have access to one at the moment.

Heart Healing Self-Reflection Exercise

This exercise is meant to help you reflect upon the energy of the heart and to help you reflect on those things in your energy that are holding you back as it pertains to loving and healthy relationships.

Just like before, you may stop anywhere along the way to pause and reflect but there are suggested areas where you can stop and reflect as well. You may choose to read each passage, stopping to visualize the suggestions along the way, or you may choose to read through the entire piece first, then go back to do the exercise. Do whatever feels comfortable for you.

Take a nice deep breath. Relax your body, starting at your face and working your way down to your toes. Take as long as you need to do this, breathing comfortably as you do.

As thoughts come to you, just acknowledge them, and let them float away. Continue to relax and slowly breathe in… and slowly exhale…. In this state, you are connecting to life's energy.

Feel yourself sinking deeper and deeper where you are, letting go of all distractions and thoughts. As you take another deep breath then slowly exhale, feel yourself growing very peaceful and centred.

Spend a few moments here before moving on to the next section.

The heart chakra is the very foundation of the astral body and in many ways it is your connection between your physical body and your spiritual body. The heart chakra is of course driven by love. The heart chakra gives you compassion, trust, empathy, equilibrium, forgiveness, love, intimacy, healthy relationships and of course that all-important concept of self-love.

The heart chakra influences the lungs, thymus, circulation and the endocrine and immune system. When the heart chakra is well balanced you are able to strike a healthy balance that allows you to experience unconditional love and harmony with others. The heart chakra helps you feel at peace with the world and with those around you. Problems in the heart chakra can cause you to feel unstable, unloved, become a martyr, become obsessed, cause you to repress emotional issues, feel indifferent, miserly, bitter and even jealous.

A heart chakra that is blocked can cause you to suppress trauma and of course cause you to have trouble experiencing the emotion of love. Issues with this chakra can also cause heart disease, diseases of the immune system and even things like chronic fatigue syndrome. An unbalanced heart chakra can cause problems in the circulatory system, the lungs and the endocrine system as well. The color pink or green is typically associated with the heart chakra.

When you feel completely relaxed, pick up your rose quartzcrystal, if you have one, and hold it between your palms. You may imagine one as well.

Now set the intent for your meditation. Affirm to yourself, out loud or in your head,

"I am now willing to allow my heart to heal. I now allow myself to move forward from the past into a better future."

Now place the rose quartz crystal against your heart chakra, right in the middle of your chest. You may of course simply visualize a rose quartz crystal if you don't access to one. You can hold it there with your hand, or just set it there if it will stay. Take another deep breath, and imagine the energy of your heart opening like a beautiful flower; visualize whatever type of flower feels right for you. As the petals open and bloom, quietly say to yourself:

"I am open to healing – I am open to healing."

Take a moment to feel how your heart chakra reacts to these statements. If you have a rose quartz crystal, or any other healing crystal, notice how the energy of the heart reacts to the stone.

In somecases, especially for those of us with self-hatred issues, the energy of this loving stone can be overwhelming. If this is the case, just place a hematite or other dark-colored stone between your feet or in your lap and leave it there during the meditation. Breathe again until you feel centered.

Spend a few moments here before moving on to the next section.

Theheart chakra opens in two directions, through both your chest and your back. Once you open the front of your heart chakra – you may then visualize another flower opening up on the center of your back. This flower may be the same or different as the flower on your chest.

Opening up both the front and back of this powerful chakra allows a greater release of blocks and negativity. As you release negativity through this meditation, the loving energy of thishealing stone will naturally move into your heart center, allowing you to mend and heal the gaps left behind, making your heart stronger and more receptive to love of all kinds.

Once both the front and back of your heart chakra is open, take another nice deep breath. Now affirm to yourself:

"I am ready to release the pain and fear that has built up in the energy of my heart. I am willing to forgive, even those who don't deserve my forgiveness. I do this for myself. I now take back my power and move forward in harmony."

Spend as much time here as you need - there is no rush; if you feel as if you have done enough work for today that's fine. You may do this meditation as often as you like. Meditate on your willingness to receive healing, and stay with the energy for a while before moving on.

Spend a few moments here before moving on to the next section.

Take a moment now to think about the people in your life who have hurt you the most. One of those people might even be you. Let yourself really feel the pain - you might be surprised at how raw it feels, no matter how much time has passed. It's important to fully experience the wounds that have been hiding in your heart chakra before you can let them go.

When you're ready, think again specifically about the people who have hurt you the most. You might be harboring bitterness, hatred, anger or resentment towards them. It's understandable; they hurt you, after all. Pay attention to how it feels to be harboring these hurtful feelings. How do these painful emotions resonate within your heart? Now shift the emotions that come up to someone or something you love - your significant other, or child; niece, nephew, even a loving pet. Feel the difference in the energy. Notice how good it would feel to release this hurtful energy, once and for all.

Visualize the pain and anger that you've been tuning into as shackles, brambles, or chains around your heart. You might even see this energy as a dark mass or a coiled energy or knotted piece of rope.

See the dark, heavy, energy the heart is holding onto.Notice and acknowledge that it's time to reclaim your personal power, and your ability to trust and love. As long as you still hate someone, they own a part of you. Make a pact right now to take that part back.

Affirm to yourself now:

"I reclaim my personal power by letting go of the pain."

Call upon your rose quartz to re-ignite the compassion and the love that has been numb in your heart.

Imagine this compassion is the color pink like your crystal. See the color flowing outward from your heart, easily dissolving the shackles or bindings that have been holding onto this vital energy center. Let the pink light grow deeper and strongeras the shackles grow smaller and weaker, or the ropes begin to unwind or even disappear. Allow your heart chakra to glow, to shine with love for yourself and the good people you have in your life.

Focus now on those loved ones, and picture them within your heart. Now picture the people that you're forgiving as well - not as they were when they hurt you, but as little children. Recognize that we've all been hurt, and the people who hurt you were more than likely hurt by others, too. Place those little children in the center of your heart, and send them all love. Hopefully someday they will also learn how to forgive and release their pain, so they may treat others better.

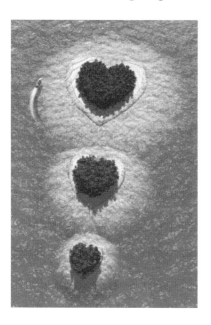

Give yourself a few minutes to breathe deeply, enjoying your expanded heart chakra and the energy flowing through it. Don't focus on anything but the way these new feelings resonate as you adjust to them. Let your rose quartz continue to energize your heart center.

When you're ready, close up the chakra flowers you envisioned on your chest and back. Take a deep breath, and rub your hands together.

Open your eyes if they were closed, and set your rose quartz aside for cleansing later. You may cleanse stones by running them through incense smoke or even beneath running water.Enjoy your newly healed heart chakra!

Feel free to do this meditation as much or as often as you like.

"Peace comes from within. Do not seek it without."
Gautama Buddha

Chapter 6: Family Relationship Patterns – Why We Emulate the One's We Love

"By nature, we are all creatures of habit.
We instinctively adopt familiar routines for most activities.
We eat about the same number of meals each day -
at more or less the same times.
We have a regular pattern of sleeping -
unless it is perturbed by illness or shift work.
Most everything we do is habitual."

- Jonathan Lockwood Huie

Thus far, you have confronted the truth mirror, acknowledged your inner child and embraced the darkness within – you have also worked with the energy of the chakras and the energy of the heart.

You may now be arriving at a point where you start looking outside of yourself for the root cause of your suffering. We often emulate the one's we love – even if we do so unconsciously. The role models we have had in our lives play a key role when it comes to relationships. If your parent's did not often show love and affection for example, you may in turn emulate those same patterns as an adult. You may then believe as a child that your parent's did not really love each other deep down which probably isn't true for the most part.

If your parent's or those adults around you did not openly express their love and affection, you will most likely grow up with the same pattern. Now having said that, don't go blaming your parent's for all of your problems, because we all make choices in our lives. Each of us is ultimately responsible for the lives we lead.

"In the long run, we shape our lives, and we shape ourselves. The process never ends until we die. And the choices we make are ultimately our own responsibility."
Eleanor Roosevelt

Each of us makes the choice every day to commit to our personal growth. All of us are constantly learning, growing and changing. The choices we make define our lives. We cannot change the choices we have already made, but we can make new choices going forward that more closely align with our dreams and goals.

The message I would like to try and portray is that each of us is the product of our own unique choices. We have no one to blame but ourselves. We cannot change the world around us but we can change how we react and we can change the choices we make from this moment forward. Each of us is empowered to make good choices or bad choices - the point is that YOU are ultimately in charge.

Many of us feel at times as if someone else is in charge of our lives and our dreams. In reality, that isn't true. The role models you have had along the way may have played a role, but you are the one that makes the choices for your life. It's OK if the role models you had growing up were not so good – just look at it as a learning experience. You can choose to react differently in your intimate relationships and you can choose to openly express your love and adoration.

You can even choose to move on or move out, if you are currently in a relationship that is not so healthy. Breaking it off with someone who is not right for you will ultimately lead both parties to a better outcome. Chances are if you are not happy with your relationship, your partner is not happy as well.

We were not put on this earth to constantly struggle. We were put on this earth to love and be loved.

Emotional Family History

Emotional family history has to do with the relational and emotional patterns that are inherited and/or learned from your parent's or even your grandparent's. These kinds of traits or patterns can be passed down to you, whether you realize it or not.

This might also be known as "nurture versus nature". Things like a predisposition to certain mental or emotional problems like depression, anxiety or addictions for example, may get passed down to you genetically. This is the nature part of the equation.

Looking at the nurture part – we see that certain patterns can also be learned. These might have to do with patterns we learn on how to handle or manage emotions in relationships or even how to express love and affection.

Looking back at your emotional family history can offer you valuable insights into why you do the things you do. Being aware of the positive traits is just as important as being aware of the negative traits.

The more you can identify certain traits the more the puzzle of your emotional life will come together. If the patterns you identify are not so positive, that's OK too. Seeing what your parent's or grandparent's or ancestors struggled with allows you to have much more empathy and awareness.

Sometimes it's hard to ask these difficult questions – but I would encourage you to seek the truth anyway. Your emotional family history is extremely valuable, and it can help you understand your own struggles.

You don't have to emulate these patterns – and as a matter of fact, knowledge is power because it allows you to seek a different path. Looking at my own family in terms of our emotional patterns, I can see that I come from a very colorful family! My father had a horrible upbringing because his own father treated him very poorly. His mother died when he was young, and his father remarried. This is the classic tale of the evil stepmother, because my own father's stepmother wanted nothing to do with him and she insisted he be kicked out of the house at 16. This is a terrible way to start your adult life, but my amazing father, who has since passed away, didn't let that stop him from being an amazing father to me. He didn't let his emotional baggage color the way he lived his life when he had his children.

Sometimes examining and identifying these patterns can be life changing - because it gives you a reason to act in a different manner, in spite of the way you grew up.

"Dance like nobody's watching; love like you've never been hurt. Sing like nobody's listening; live like it's heaven on earth." - Mark Twain

In my last book, "Change Anything by Overcoming Fear" I talked of the idea that each of us are merely actors on our own stage of life – and that analogy still applies when it comes to relationships.

In other words, if you do what you have always done, you will most likely get what you have always gotten! In the end, you are the only one that can change your life. You are the director, the producer, the actor and even the stage hand in your play of life. If you don't like the path that you have been on, it may be high time to re-examine the way you live your life and it may be time to re-examine the choices you make from here on out.

Embracing change and owning your own faults and mishaps is emotionally freeing. It's sometimes fun to just admit that you don't know what you are doing. It's even OK to admit that you have made poor choices along the way; just the fact that you have recognized that your choices have not been so great, puts you ahead of the game.

My cousin once told my sister and I "our pickers were broken". She said it out of love, but she had a good point. Just acknowledging the fact that we obviously had a history of making poor choices when it came to men gave us a good laugh. Sometimes it's good to laugh at yourself because it reminds you to lighten up.

Life shouldn't be so hard, and as a matter of fact, it should be joyful.

If there is a part of your life that is not joyful, you have the power to change it. It doesn't matter what you have done up to this point, what does matter is what you do from this moment forward.Remember, people come into your life for a reason, a season or a lifetime.

Chapter 7: Are You Ready for a Healthy Relationship –Moving Into a Space of Love

"Our deepest fear is not that we are inadequate. Our deepest fear is that we are powerful beyond measure. It is our light, not our darkness that most frightens us. We ask ourselves, 'Who am I to be brilliant, gorgeous, talented, fabulous?' Actually, who are you not to be? You are a child of God. Your playing small does not serve the world."- Marianne Williamson

I love this quote because it is very empowering. If you are embroiled in a toxic relationship, or in a toxic relationship cycle you may not see yourself as brilliant, gorgeous, talented or fabulous when in fact, we are ALL brilliant, talented, gorgeous and fabulous.

Being in a toxic relationship can be very draining; it can suck the life right out of you if you allow it to. You may see yourself in this book in some way shape or form. Each of us has different degrees of toxic patterns to some extent, because we are after all only human.

Sometimes, the best way to get out of a toxic cycle is to simply take a time out as far as relationships go. It's not always necessary to be in a relationship. Taking time out for yourself may be the perfect solution for you at this moment in time. It is not selfish to do so but you may find that your family and friends don't quite understand why you have chosen not to date. Everyone will be encouraging you to get back out there! They may mean well, but sometimes it is just necessary to take a break from life.

Spending time on your own for a few months can be emotionally freeing. It gives you time to rediscover who you really are and what you really want from a relationship. Your biggest problem may then become trying to stay out of a relationship, because when you are sending out the vibe that you are not interested, people flock to you.

When you are not encumbered with a relationship, you can focus on YOU. You can also take some time to discover what your pattern is and why you have been following it. You may discover that you are trying to recreate the same kind of patterns that you experienced growing up. It's not uncommon for women to seek partners just like their father or grandfather in my case.

The good news is that now that you have acknowledge the fact that you are in this toxic pattern, you can now take steps to get out of the pattern. You can't help yourself if you don't realize you have this tendency.

Relationships are a lot like plants in many ways, if we feed them and love them and care for them they thrive; if we neglect them or ignore them they grow wild or lose their will to survive.

Relationships can be thrilling and exhilarating or they can be toxic and draining. Some relationships build us up while others tear us down. Some relationships take no effort whatsoever while others are nothing but hard work.

We were not meant to live our lives completely alone because we are not islands but relationships can definitely test our patience. You will experience many different types of relationships during the course of your life - and they all require time and effort and commitment.

Relationships are what make the world go around, but they take effort and patience and determination. Sometimes we determine that our relationships are just too much work and we choose to abandon them or betray them. In the ideal world, relationships would be effortless and they would build us up each and every day. In the real world, relationships can be very challenging to say the least. Relationships can test our patience and test our friendships.

There are many different types of relationships including parental relationships, work relationships, love relationships, and even family relationships. There are many different levels of relationships. Some people come into our lives for a reason or a season and then quietly fade away. Others stay in the background and surface only when we need them. They say one is lucky to have one really good friend in their lifetime and I have to say I agree with that. It is not always necessary to have hoards of friends unless that is your choice. A good friend is always there when you need them and they never judge you, no matter what.

Relationships can be the bane of our existence or the light of our lives but in the end relationships matter. Think about all of those people in your life who build you up. There are those in our lives whose energy we crave; the kinds of people whom we can't wait to be around – on the other hand, there are those whose energy drains us. What determines which one someone is? Why are some relationships so difficult while others are so easy? What is it that turns a relationship sour? People learn and change and grow at different rates and this can affect our relationships. We all grow at different paces and sometimes we outgrow our relationships. Some relationships are meant to last a lifetime while others are often over before they even get started.

The best kind of relationship takes no effort whatsoever, it just is. It's nice to be around someone who just lets you be you, no matter what. These kinds of relationships can be difficult to find, but once you find one, they are worth their weight in gold. These kinds of relationships stay with us for a lifetime and their memories never fade or weaken no matter how far apart one may be.

Relationships take hard work and time and commitment and often the most difficult ones to maintain are the relationships within our own family. Feelings get hurt and people hold grudges and many of us find it difficult to let go and forgive and forget. Even though relationships can be challenging, they sustain us and help us get through difficult times. They are there for us to lean on whenever we need them. The best kinds of relationships complement one another much like the yin and the yang. Some people are just meant for each other and you can feel it the moment you connect with them. We may have a kind of magical connection with some, andfind someone else fights with us at every turn.

Without the pain of a difficult relationship, one may not appreciate an effortless one quite so much. Relationships make our lives better in every single way and we never ever lose hope as long as someone is there to offer a kind shoulder or a warm embrace. Relationships make our lives interesting and they often make life worth living. Relationships offer us many things including companionship, friendship, and even love.

Don't ever forget what it is that you have to offer. Your life has meaning and you matter because you are someone's friend, lover, companion and child.

Relationships are beautiful, meaningful and purposeful and we will always be part of one in some way shape or form whether it's as a mother, a father, a lover or a friend. Relationships are worth the effort so don't ever forget to feed and care for yours the best you know how.

There are so many good and decent people out there that you may be surprised at what you find when you do decide to jump back into the relationship game. When you are empowered with knowledge, you will be able to quickly see the warning signs if you happen to date someone who expresses any of these tendencies. Make a point to go slow, there is no rush. Choose to not become intimate with someone until you are absolutely sure it's what you want. This gives you much more freedom of choice.

Know in your mind that you have a "zero tolerance" policy for any kind of abusive or controlling behavior, and set clear ground rules.

It's much easier to step out of a relationship early on than to keep it going and try to step out later when you are much more emotionally involved.

Take time every day to envision exactly the type of person and relationship you want. You might even choose to make a handwritten list of the characteristics you are seeking in a love match. In essence, you are placing an order to the Universe by doing this.

If you become that which you continually focus on, the more you visualize and fill your mind with the thoughts of a healthy, loving relationship, the faster you will draw that relationship to you. Your relationship should be your pride and joy. It should build you up and inspire you. You should look forward to going home at night and cuddling with your sweetie, because you deserve the absolute best. Relationships shouldn't take up all of your time and effort either - it's good to strive for a healthy balance. If you trust someone, there is no reason to be jealous. I love this quote someone shared with me on Facebook:

"Disappointments are just God's way of saying 'I've got something better.' Be patient, live life, have faith."

It's important to associate with people that inspire you and to associate with people that challenge you to rise higher. Don't waste your valuable time with anyone that doesn't resonate with your energy. Your destiny is too important.

I will end this chapter with this beautiful quote from Will Smith. It encapsulates what I am trying to say.

"Don't chase people. Be yourself, do your own thing, and work hard. The right people – the one's who really belong in your life – will come to you. And stay."- Will Smith

I couldn't have said it better myself. As for my own personal journey, I am still learning, growing and changing each and every day. I am what you could call a work in progress. One thing I do know is that I will never stop hoping and dreaming of that perfect life and that perfect relationship.

"When everything seems to fall apart, that's when everything new that you prayed for has room to enter your life." Doreen Virtue

Chapter 8: Meditation for Manifesting Love

This exercise is meant to help you reflect upon the energy of love. The basic Law of Attraction states that you will attract to you those things and people that match your beliefs.

"God, grant me the serenity to accept the things I cannot change, the courage to change the things I can, and the wisdom to know the difference." – Serenity Prayer

Believing that your perfect partner is out there is critical to this preparation. The Universe always mirrors back to you your beliefs about yourself and the world. If you believe the world is a friendly and loving place, then that will be your experience most of the time. On the other hand, if you believe the world is a stressful and traumatic place, then those fears will eventually become your new reality. Believing and knowing that your ideal partner and your ideal relationshipis out there is the most important part of this process.

Just like before, you may stop anywhere along the way to pause and reflect but there are suggested areas where you can stop and reflect as well. You may choose to read each passage, stopping to visualize the suggestions along the way, or you may choose to read through the entire piece first, then go back to do the exercise. Do whatever feels comfortable for you.

Don't get overly concerned with trying to figure out exactly HOW and WHEN your perfect partner or relationship is going to appear.

This exercise will help you so that you are ready, willing and open to love.

Love has really always been there - you just need to remember the love that you hold in your heart and the love you feel inside yourself. The moment you do this and become content with who you are deep down inside, is the moment you let your guard down and allow the Universe to deliver what it is your heart desires.

You might want to have your list handy of the traits and characteristics you are looking for in an ideal relationship so that you can focus on it during this exercise. If you haven't done so yet, now is the perfect time to stop and reflect on exactly what it is you are seeking.

Create a "vision" or list of your romantic vision and focus on it. Write a list of the most important qualities you are seeking for in a person so that you can focus on it during this exercise. Try and focus on those inner qualities rather than the exterior "façade".

Spend a few moments doing this before moving on to the next section.

Take a deep breath in and drink in the calm - imagine every fiber, every cell and every muscle of your body simply melting away.Now in this beautiful state of peace, visualize a cleansing and healing white light streaming down from above. Feel this light wash over you, cleansing your energy. Now focus your attention on this feeling of relaxation and allow it to filter through to all of the muscles as if you were taking a shower of pure white light. Now allow this feeling of deep relaxation to flow into the muscles of your body,working your way from top to bottom, and then back up again.

Allow this wonderful feeling of heaviness to gently wash over you like a gentle stream of water. Feel this stream running down over your arms, and out through your fingers and let the softness just take over. Now move this relaxation down to your feet and toes, feeling the heaviness as it takes over - until all of the stress and tension in your entire body drains down and out through the ends of your toes. See your energy grounded, as if your feet were connected to a long, intertwining system of roots, that connect deep into the ground.

With each inhale of breath, you are drawing in energy, and as you exhale, that energy is spreading and vibrating throughout your entire body. Keep breathing in and out until this life energy leaves you tingling. Now, take a deep breath in and send all this beautiful life energy upwards. Release the breath and feel the life energy rising above you. Ask for whatever it is you need at this moment. Feel the love that is all around you. Let it surround you and fill you. Stay with these feelings for as long as you need, there is no rush and you are in no hurry. Feel this divine connection, that which connects you to the divine spirit within yourself and know that you are loved, no matter what.

Spend a few moments doing this before moving on to the next section.

When you make decisions that come from your heart, you are aligning yourself with your highest goals and values. Learning how to connect with your heart gives your life meaning and value and purpose. Connecting with your heart means to dig down deep inside yourself and discover what makes your heart sing. Emotions like love and friendship and pleasure giveyour life meaning.

The emotion of love heals us and makes us whole; it is our connection to the divine and our connection to others. The heart chakra is located in the very center of your energetic body, and it helps you make the connection from the earth down below and the sky up above. When your emotions are tied up in hate and anger and resentment, your energy gets blocked. When your energy is blocked, it keeps you from being the best you can be.

Take a moment now to release any negative or bitter feelings you may be holding onto as it pertains to love. These feelings no longer resonate with your energy. Watch them as they float out of your body, out into the world.

The heart's electromagnetic field generated by your heartbeat forms an energetic field that connects you to your higher power or higher self and it also connects you to others. The heart's energy is very powerful. When you are really clear about what you want out of life, the Universe conspires to help you obtain it. Connecting with your heart means you are being true to who you really are, at the deepest level of your being. Connecting with your heart also helps you better align with those things you feel passionate about and those things that inspire you.

When you learn how to let go and let your heart lead, it frees you to let love in. The power of divine love heals all and it has immense healing properties. Love is the glue that holds us together and love is the reason we go on. Without love, our lives have little meaning and without love, we cannot connect with our heart.

Leslie D Riopel

As you learn to connect with your heart, you can begin to build a powerful healing relationship with yourself and the people in your life.

Imagine now how the energy of your heart feels. You may experience it as a beautiful color or a type of energy or pulse. Feel the energy all around you. Consider that you radiate – at all times. Whenever you are focused on feelings of love, that love surrounds you and emanates from you.

Focus on something positive for a moment. This might be a happy experience, the love of a child or even a pet. Feel how good this person or thing makes you feel. Now focus on how you feel about your place in the world as it pertains to love and affection. Are you happy and content or do you feel as if you could stand some improvement as it pertains to love and companionship? Know that there is always room for improvement.

The emotion of love is an untapped resource and there is plenty to go around.

Contemplate love for a moment, and imagine your heart as a beautiful flower, opening up to the world. See the colors in the area of the heart opening and spinning in a healthy manner. See it spinning away anything that no longer serves you, like a centrifuge.

Imagine this energy is growing until it becomes larger than you. Now send this energy out into the world, and watch as it moves and grows. Now ask yourself how much you really love yourself for exactly who you are? Your standards for love should be extremely high, because you deserve the absolute best. Know that anyone would be extraordinarily grateful and lucky to be with you.

Now think about those qualities you seek in a person now, what kind of personality do you look for? If you are already in a loving relationship, think about those ways that you could express your love more kindly and more genuinely. Relationships are always ebbing and flowing, so they require care and upkeep. It's important to keep things fresh and vibrant. If you have been stuck in a negative or toxic pattern, you can release those tendencies right now, because they no longer serve you.

If you are seeking love, try and see yourself from an outside perspective. Do you give off the energy of love? Are you open to love and companionship? Are you a good receiver of love? If not, change that dynamic right now.Embrace yourself and your life flaws and all. See yourself as beautifully flawed but perfect in every way. Your quirks make you unique and special. There is no one else on earth quite like you.

Now focus on those qualities you desire in someone. See those qualities come to life. Focus on the kind of person you desire. Focus on the energy of a positive and loving relationship. How would this kind of relationship make you feel? Focus on those feelings. You might think about someone who is kind, loving, respectful, genuine, caring or even someone who is passionate. Whatever qualities you desire, think about them now.

Spend a few moments doing this before moving on to the next section.

Now see yourself sitting in a beautiful gazebo out in the country. Imagine it is a warm summer day, and the air smells sweet. Feel the sun on your skin, and feel the invigorating energy. See yourself sitting here, in this gazebo. You might imagine the feeling you get when you go on vacation or take a day off. See yourself just sitting here relaxing, and enjoying the day.

Now focus on someone now that you would like to attract. This might be someone new, someone you have never met or someone you need to make amends with. Welcome this person, or this companion, up into the gazebo and show them some affection. Show them how much you care and how much you appreciate them. Take this time right now. Do not hold anything back.

Take this time to sit and reflect. See yourself in a happy conversation with this person. Imagine them sitting there right next to you laughing and smiling. Who is it you see? What do they look like? What does their energy feel like? This might be an entirely new feeling, just enjoy it. This is a happy time, a pleasant experience - there is no rush - no pressure, just friendship and laughter and joy.

You may sit here as long as you like, as long as you need.

If you are with someone new, just give him or her a peck on the cheek or give him or her a casual hug, from one friend to another. Sit and chat for a while and just enjoy the day. Show someone the love you are capable of. Imagine your heart is radiating out a lovely green energy, the energy of love. This is a place of immense healing and you can use this time any way you like.

Now see the energy of this positive relationship growing and expanding all around you. See it like a bubble of energy moving out into the world. Watch as the energy grows ten times it's normal size. See it as mist or cloud of beautiful light around you. Imagine this energy is growing, beyond the gazebo, beyond your immediate surroundings, beyond the skies. Infuse this energy with the qualities you seek in someone and send this energy out into the world.

Allow it to work its magic in the coming days and the coming weeks. Allow love to heal and transform your life, in whatever way it needs to.

As you return to conscious awareness, know that you are loved, because you are love. Take time each and every day to focus on those qualities you seek in a loving and compassionate partner.

I hope you enjoyed this book. I will end it with this beautiful quote by Patrick Overton.

"When you walk to the edge of all the light you have and take that first step into the darkness of the unknown, you must believe that one of two things will happen. There will be something solid for you to stand upon or you will be taught to fly."

I hope you choose to fly. I wish you much luck in the journey ahead. May you find love, and peace and joy in your heart. Remember, you deserve the best.

"I am enough of an artist to draw freely upon my imagination. Imagination is more important than knowledge. Knowledge is limited. Imagination encircles the world." —

Albert Einstein.

Disclaimer Notice:

Please note the information contained within this document is for educational purposes only.
Every attempt has been made to provide accurate, up-to-date, and reliable complete information. No warranties of any kind are expressed or implied. Readers acknowledge that the author is not engaging in rendering legal, financial, or professional advice.

By reading any document, the reader agrees that under no circumstances are we responsible for any losses, direct or indirect, which are incurred as a result of use of the information contained within this document, including but not limited to errors, omissions, or inaccuracies.

References:

http://www.scribd.com/doc/105084129/Dr-Seth-s-Love-Prescription-Overcome-Relationship-Repetition-Syndrome-and-Find-the-Love-You-Deserve\

http://www.psychologytoday.com/blog/evil-deeds/200806/essential-secrets-psychotherapy-repetitive-relationship-patterns

http://psychcentral.com/blog/archives/2013/06/29/repetition-compulsion-why-do-we-repeat-the-past/

http://beautifulquotestoliveby.blogspot.com/2008/04/people-come-into-your-life-for-reason.html

http://www.boardofwisdom.com/togo/Quotes/ShowQuote?msgid=408435#.U1_ZiLpdWQs

http://www.juliehanks.com/tag/family-relationship-patterns/

http://www.healthscopemag.com/toxic-relationships/

Leslie D Riopel

Printed in Great Britain
by Amazon